This Cats' Eye View book belongs to

Dedicated to our girls

Special thanks to:

My fabulous editor Tonie Lambie,
'Wyatt & Jack' and 'Chilly's Bottles'
for their lovely photographs,
and the wonderful @CleanUpTadworth
for their photo - and all their hard work.

Copyright © 2022 Octavia Lonergan.

All rights reserved. This book or any portion thereof
may not be reproduced or used in any manner whatsoever
without the express written permission of the author
except for the use of brief quotations in a book review.

Cats' Eye View of BEING GREEN

Written & illustrated by Octavia Lonergan

Mimi, looking rather **tired** ... lets out such a **yawn**.

Yesterday, the cats all talked of **litter** in the park... Mimi **worried** - up all night. Everything looked dark!

" It seems some **humans** aren't aware - the **mess** we could get in - dropping **rubbish** on the ground instead of in the **bin**. "

"It needn't be all **doom** and **gloom**, dear Mimi - do not stress. There's **lots** of things that they can do to **clean up** all this mess."

Leo joins in with the chat
as something rings a bell...
(a cheeky little ginger cat,
but curious as well)

"Speaking of a **rubbish** bin
I've seen there's more than one.
Different bins for different things
it looks like **lots** of **fun!**"

"Ah yes, they're called **recycling** bins"
the cats hear Ozzy shout
"that's one way that the humans try
to **help** our planet out."

" They separate the different bits like **tins** and **glass** and **plastic** (before it's binned they check that it is nice and clean, for sure)

And then before you know it - this part is quite **fantastic** - a recycled thing is made from what was thrown away before! "

So, how many recycling bins do you have at home? What do you put in each one?

" There are many ways to **change** stuff into different items, too - **shopping bags** from bouncy castles, cards from **elephant poo!**

Can you draw me a picture of a new thing you've made from something that was going to be thrown away? Send it to @poemsbyoctavia

Dusters made from **socks** - **chairs** from a wheelbarrow?

Or maybe make a **plant pot** from a **welly** that's too narrow?! "

"I heard my humans talking
about throwing things away;
and that it's bad if they don't **try**
to find **another** way!

They want to be **less** wasteful –
and if something breaks, they'll **mend** it,
buy things **secondhand**... or see
if someone else can lend it."

" They sometimes **freeze** the food that's left
to eat another **day**,
or put scraps in their **compost** bin -
yes, that's **another** way!

The plastic straws they **used** to have
to sip their favourite drink,
have been replaced by **special** ones -
they **wash** them in the sink! "

What can you put into a compost or food waste bin? What has to go into a different one?

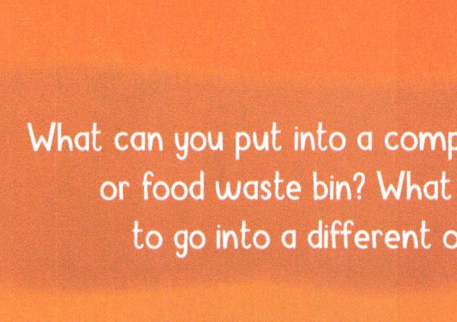

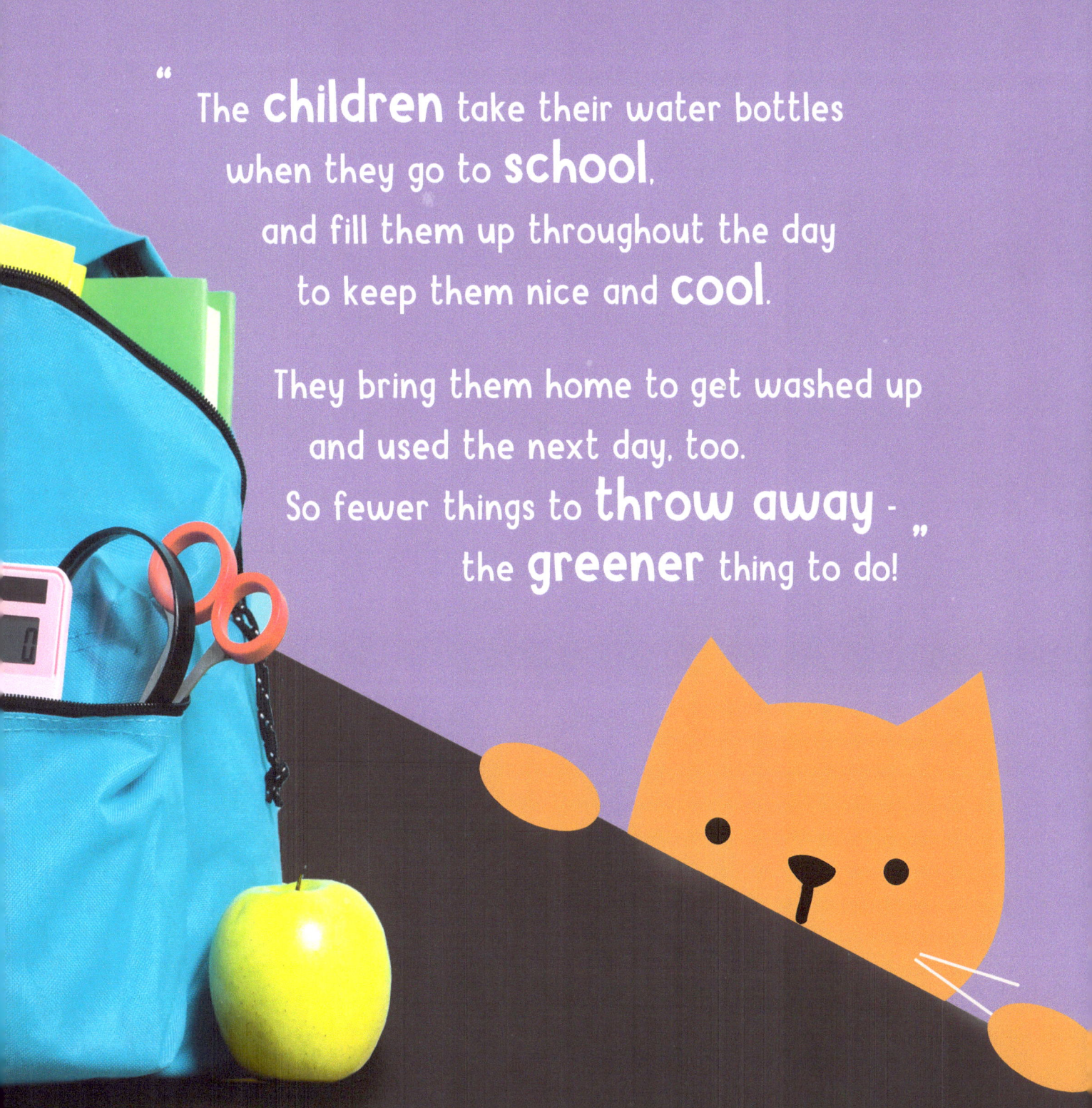

"The **children** take their water bottles
when they go to **school**,
and fill them up throughout the day
to keep them nice and **cool**.

They bring them home to get washed up
and used the next day, too.
So fewer things to **throw away** -
the **greener** thing to do!"

" The humans wear their **jumpers**
before they turn the **heat** up -

to get all nice and **cosy**
before they put their **feet** up!

They usually keep their doors shut in **winter** when it's **chilly** which helps to keep the **warmth** inside – that's certainly **not** silly! "

What other ways can you think of to keep it warm indoors?

"My humans turn the lights out when they leave the room, even when I'm sitting there - I get left in the gloom!

They make a point of switching off the **telly** when they go, even **if** it's in the middle of my favourite show! "

"They always **turn off** all their taps, they say that it **saves water**.

I heard the lady human explain it to her daughter."

What other ways can you save water at home?

" The **cars** and **trucks** they drive can cause
a problem called **pollution**,
when dirty fumes go up into the air

Thank **goodness** there are people
who've worked out some great solutions
that help to **save the Earth**,
and show they care.

In some towns there are areas where owners have to pay to drive a car that's **really** bad - it keeps the **worst** away!"

" Some people drive **electric** cars,
and others ride a **bike**.
Or if it isn't too far they can
walk there if they like.

There's something called an **e-bike**
and pedaling is the power.
The rider can get really far
in **only half an hour!** "

"Or using **public** transport like a bus, tube, train or tram, causes **less** pollution – fewer **cars** to cause a jam!"

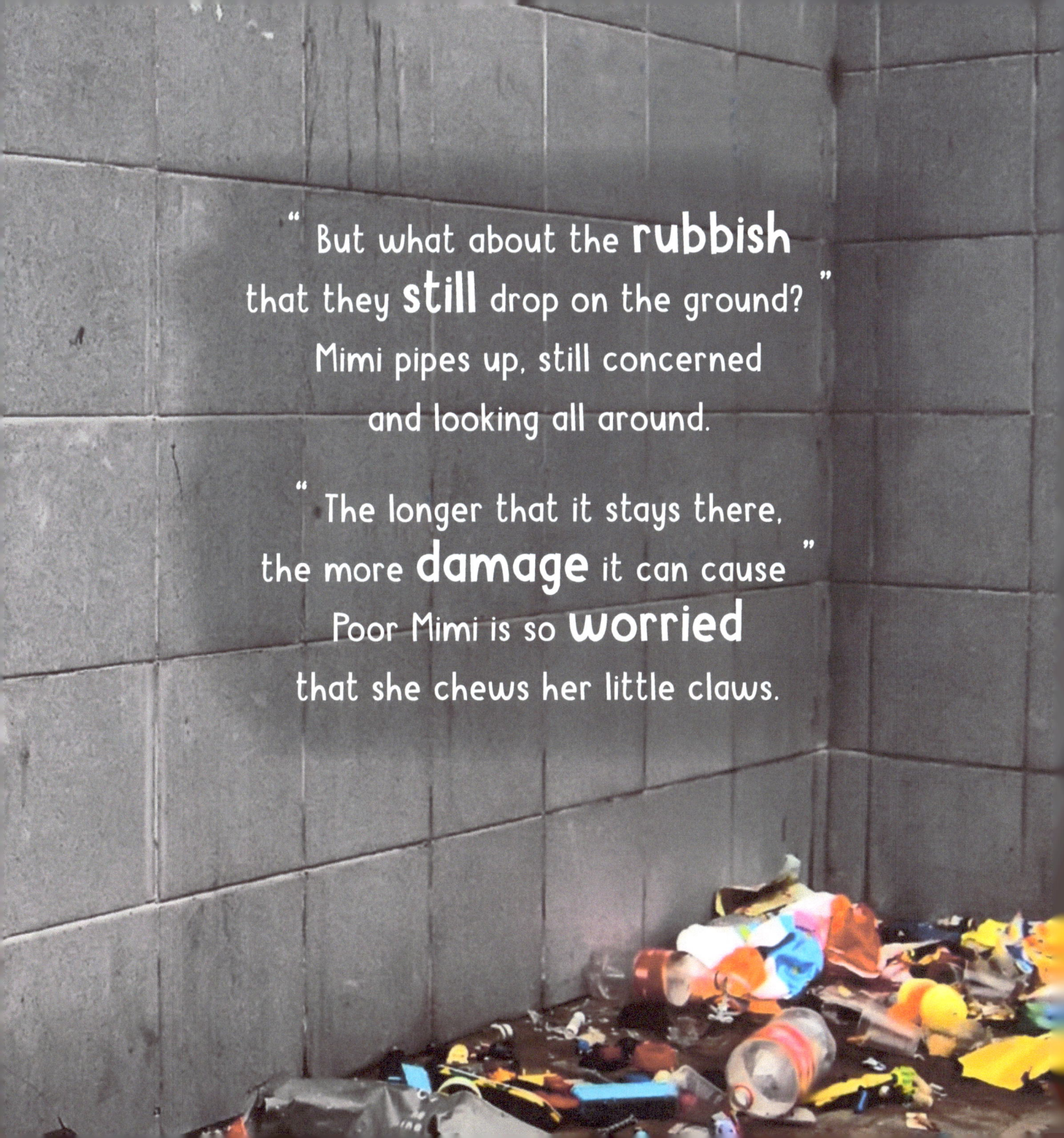

" But what about the **rubbish**
that they **still** drop on the ground? "
Mimi pipes up, still concerned
and looking all around.

" The longer that it stays there,
the more **damage** it can cause "
Poor Mimi is so **worried**
that she chews her little claws.

About the Author

Octavia's love of writing poems stretches back to childhood, along with a passion for creating art and music. In 2020 she finally realised her dream of becoming a children's author.

Also a graphic designer with over 20 years' professional experience, Octavia lives in Surrey, England with her husband, and their twin daughters - her inspiration and motivation.

Learn more at poemsbyoctavia.com

If you've enjoyed this book, please do leave a review!
Just scan the QR code below.

Next in the series...

Cats' Eye View of Kindness

To keep up-to-date follow
@poemsbyoctavia on social media